MW01519024

WINTER

First published in the United States by
Salem House Publishers, 462 Boston Street,
Topsfield, Massachusetts, 01983.

Copyright © Swallow Publishing Ltd 1988

Conceived and produced by
Swallow Publishing Ltd, Swallow House,
11-21 Northdown Street, London N1 9BN

ISBN: 0 88162 341 5
Art Director: Elaine Partington
Designer: Jean Hoyes
Printed in Hong Kong by Imago Publishing Limited

KEEPSAKES
WINTER

Compiled by
Kenneth Deare

Salem House

Nightly Sings the Owl

When icicles hang by the wall,
    And Dick the shepherd blows his nail,
And Tom bears logs into the hall,
    And milk comes frozen home in pail,
When blood is nipp'd, and ways be foul,
    Then nightly sings the staring owl, Tu-who;
Tu-whit, tu-who – a merry note,
    While greasy Joan doth keel the pot.

When all aloud the wind doth blow,
    And coughing drowns the parson's saw,
And birds sit brooding in the snow,
    And Marian's nose looks red and raw,
When roasted crabs hiss in the bowl,
    Then nightly sings the staring owl, Tu-who;
Tu-whit, tu-who – a merry note,
    While greasy Joan doth keel the pot.

WILLIAM SHAKESPEARE

SNOWY OWL.

Through the Hushed Air

Through the hushed air the whitening shower descends,
    At first thin-wavering, till at last the flakes
Fall broad, and wide, and fast, dimming the day
    With a continual flow. The cherished fields
Put on their winter robe of purest white.
    'Tis brightness all, save where the snow melts,
Along the mazy current. Lo, the woods
    Bow their hoar head; and ere the languid sun
Faint from the west emits his evening ray,
    Earth's universal face, deep-hid, and chill,
Is one wild dazzling waste, that buries deep
    The works of man. Drooping, the labourer-ox
Stands covered o'er with snow, and then demands
    The fruit of all his toil. The fowls of heaven,
Tamed by the cruel season, crowd around
    The winnowing store, and claim the little boon
Which providence assigns them. One alone,
    The Redbreast, sacred to the household gods,
Wisely regardful of the embroiling sky,
    In joyless fields and thorny thickets leaves
His shivering mates, and pays to trusted man
    His annual visit.

ELIZABETH TOLLET

A HAPPY NEW YEAR

The Darkling Thrush

I leant upon a coppice gate
    When Frost was spectre-grey,
And Winter's dregs made desolate
    The weakening eye of day.
The tangled bine-stems scored the sky
    Like strings of broken lyres,
And all mankind that haunted nigh
    Had sought their household fires.

At once a voice arose among
    The bleak twigs overhead
In a full-hearted evensong
    Of joy illimited;
An aged thrush, frail, gaunt, and small
    In blast-beruffled plume,
Had chosen thus to fling his soul
    Upon the growing gloom.

THOMAS HARDY

Feeling the Cold

FEBRUARY MORNING, windy, cold, with chill-looking clouds hurrying over a pale sky and chill snow-drops for sale in the grey streets.... Flinging her small scarf over her shoulder again, clasping her violin, Miss Bray darts along to orchestra practice. She is conscious of her cold hands, her cold nose and her colder feet. She can't feel her toes at all. Her feet are just little slabs of cold, all of a piece, like the feet of china dolls. Winter is a terrible time for thin people – terrible! Why should it hound them down, fasten on them, worry them so? Why not, for a change, take a nip, take a snap at the fat ones who wouldn't notice? But no! It is sleek, warm, cat-like summer that makes the fat one's life a misery. Winter is all for bones....

Threading her way, like a needle, in and out and along, went Miss Bray, and she thought of nothing but the cold. She had just come out of her kitchen, which was pleasantly snug in the morning, with her gas-fire going for her break-fast and the window closed. She had just drunk three large cups of really boiling tea. Surely, they ought to have warmed her. One always read in books of people going on their way warmed and invigorated by even one cup. And she had had three!

KATHERINE MANSFIELD

Nature's Winter Dress

And yet but lately have I seen, e'en here,
    The winter in a lovely dress appear.
E'er yet the clouds let fall the treasured snow,
    Or winds begun through hazy skies to blow.
At evening a keen eastern breeze arose
    And the descending rain unsullied froze.
Soon as the silent shades of night withdrew,
    The ruddy morn disclosed at once to view
The face of nature in a rich disguise,
    And brightened every object to my eyes.
For every shrub and every blade of grass,
    And every pointed thorn, seemed wrought in glass.
In pearls and rubies rich the hawthorns show,
    While through the ice the crimson berries glow.
The thick-sprung reeds the watery marshes yield,
    Seem polished lances in a hostile field.
The stag in limpid currents with surprise
    Sees crystal branches on his forehead rise.
The spreading oak, the beech, and towering pine,
    Glazed over, in the freezing ether shine.
The frightened birds the rattling branches shun,
    That wave and glitter in the distant sun.

AMBROSE PHILIPS

Mid-Winter Carol

In the bleak mid-winter,
   Frosty wind made moan,
Earth stood hard as iron,
   Water like a stone;
Snow had fallen, snow on snow,
   Snow on snow,
In the bleak mid-winter,
   Long ago.

Our God, heaven cannot hold Him,
   Nor earth sustain;
Heaven and earth shall flee away
   When He comes to reign:
In the bleak mid-winter
   A stable-place sufficed
The Lord God Almighty,
   Jesus Christ.

CHRISTINA GEORGINA ROSSETTI

Stirrings of Life

HERE ARE FEW hedges so thick but that in January it is possible to see through them, frost and wind having brought down the leaves. The nettles, however, and coarse grasses, dry brown stems of dead plants, rushes, and moss still in some sense cover the earth of the mound, and among them the rabbits sit out in their forms. Looking for these with gun and spaniel, when the damp mist of the morning has cleared, one sign – one promise – of the warm days to come may chance to be found. Though the sky be gloomy, the hedge bare, and the trees gaunt, yet among the bushes a solitary green leaf has already put forth. It is on the stalk of the woodbine which climbs up the hawthorn, and is the first in the new year – in the very darkest and blackest days – to show that life is stirring. As it is the first to show a leaf, so, too, it is one of the latest to yield to the advancing cold, and even then its bright red berries leave a speck of colour; and its bloom, in beauty of form, hue, and fragrance, is not easily surpassed. While the hedges are so bare the rabbits are unmercifully ferreted, for they will before long begin to breed.

RICHARD JEFFERIES

The Snow Descending

Out of the bosom of the Air,
    Out of the cloud-folds of her garments shaken,
Over the woodlands brown and bare,
    Over the harvest-fields forsaken,
        Silent, and soft, and slow
        Descends the snow.

Even as our cloudy fancies take
    Suddenly shape in some divine expression,
Even as the troubled heart doth make
    In the white countenance confession,
        The troubled sky reveals
        The grief it feels.

This is the poem of the air,
    Slowly in silent syllables recorded;
This is the secret of despair,
    Long in its cloudy bosom hoarded,
        Now whispered and revealed
        To wood and field.

HENRY WADSWORTH LONGFELLOW

One Last Beauty

 N THE WINTER one last beauty comes. The day has been leaden, sad-coloured, bitterly cold. All the cab-men on the rank stamp with their feet, and swing their arms to keep themselves warm, and there is a little mist where all the horses breathe. And people coming through the square have forgotten the almond tree, and the look of the big trees when the hot sun splashed gold on their leaves, and they say, looking at the sky, 'See how dark it is, it is going to snow.' The snow comes; the sky is darker; the trees stick up looking black, like drawings in pen and ink. Flakes, white flakes, twenty, forty, then a rush – a thousand; the sky full of tiny white flakes, the air full of them whirling down. All sounds begin to be muffled. Horses hoofs beat with a thud on the ground. The sound of voices in the air is deadened. The voices of men encouraging horses sound sharp now and again, or a whip cracks like a shot. The square is covered with snow, every twig is outlined in white, black patches of bark show here and there, and emphasise the dead whiteness. When it has stopped snowing and a watery light comes from the sun all the trees gleam wonderfully, looking like fairy trees. And people passing through the square making beaten tracks in the snow saying, 'It is winter.'

DION CLAYTON CALTHROP

Rural Chores

The thresher first through darkness deep
   Awakes the morning's winter sleep,
Scaring the owlet from her prey
   Long before she dreams of day.
And foddering boys sojourn again
   By rime-hung hedge and frozen plain,
Shuffling through the sinking snows,
   Blowing his fingers as he goes
To where the stock in bellowings hoarse
   Call for their meals in dreary close,
And print full many a hungry track
   Round circling hedge that guards the stack.
With higgling tug he cuts the hay
   And bares the forkfull loads away,
And morn and evening daily throws
   The little heaps upon the snows.
The shepherd too in great coat wrapped
   And straw bands round his stockings lapped,
With plodding dog that sheltering, steals
   To shun the wind behind his heels,
Takes rough and smooth the winter weather
   And paces through the snow together.

JOHN CLARE

Winter Brilliance

Last of flowers in tufts around
   Shines the gorse's golden bloom.
Milk-white lichens clothe the ground
   'Mid the flowerless heath and broom.
Bright are holly-berries, seen
   Red, through leaves of glossy green.

Brightly, as on rocks they leap,
   Shine the sea-waves, white with spray.
Brightly, in the dingles deep,
   Gleams the river's foaming way;
Brightly through the distance show
   Mountain summits clothed in snow.

Brightly, where the torrents bound,
   Shines the frozen colonnade,
Which the black rocks, dripping round,
   And the flying spray have made.
Bright the ice-drops on the ash
   Leaning o'er the cataract's dash.

THOMAS LOVE PEACOCK

Bite, Frost, Bite!

The frost is here,
   The fuel is dear,
And woods are sear,
   And fires burn clear,
And frost is here
   And has bitten the heel of the going year.

Bite, frost, bite!
   You roll up away from the light,
The blue-wood-louse and the plump dormouse,
   And the bees are stilled and the flies are killed,
And you bite far into the heart of the house,
   But not into mine.

Bite, frost, bite!
   The woods are all the searer,
The fuel is all the dearer,
   The fires are all the clearer,
My spring is all the nearer,
   You have bitten into the heart of the earth,
But not into mine.

LORD TENNYSON

Keeping Warm and Dry

ANUARY 1901. The winter, which so far had been mild and open, began to assume its natural character with the new year; and on the first Monday of January – it was the 7th – we had snow, followed by hard frost. The snow was not unexpected. Saturday – a day of white haze suffused with sunlight – had provided a warning of it in the shape of frozen rime, clinging like serried rows of penknife blades to the eastern edges of all things, and noticeably to the telegraph-wires, which with that additional weight kept up all day a shiver of vibration dazzling to look at against the misty blue of the sky. Then the snow came, and the frost on top of that . . . .

Bettesworth grumbled, of course; but I believe that really he rather liked the touch of winter. At any rate, it was with a sort of gloating satisfaction that he remarked: 'I hunted out my old gaiters this morning. They en't much, but they keeps your legs dry. And I do think that is so nice, to feel the bottoms of your trousers dry.' I suppose it is, when one thinks of it, though it had never struck me before . . . . 'I've knowed what it is,' he said, 'to have my trousers soppin' wet all round the bottoms, and then it have come on an' freezed 'em as stiff as boards all round.'

GEORGE BOURNE

Thorough Misery

 THAW, BY ALL that is miserable! The frost is completely broken up. You look down the long perspective of Oxford Street, the gas-lights mournfully reflected on the wet pavement, and can discern no speck in the road to encourage the belief that there is a cab or a coach to be had – the very coachmen have gone home in despair. The cold sleet is drizzling down with that gentle regularity which betokens a duration of four-and-twenty hours at least; the damp hangs upon the housetops and lamp-posts, and clings to you like an invisible cloak. The water is 'coming in' in every area, the pipes have burst, the water-butts are running over; the kennels seem to be doing matches against time, pump-handles descend of their own accord, horses in market-carts fall down, and there's no one to help them up again; policemen look as if they had been carefully sprinkled with powdered glass; here and there a milk-woman trudges slowly along, with a bit of list round each foot to keep her from slipping; boys who 'don't sleep in the house,' can't wake their masters by thundering at the shop-door, and cry with the cold – the compound of ice, snow, and water on the pavement is a couple of inches thick – nobody ventures to walk fast to keep himself warm.

CHARLES DICKENS

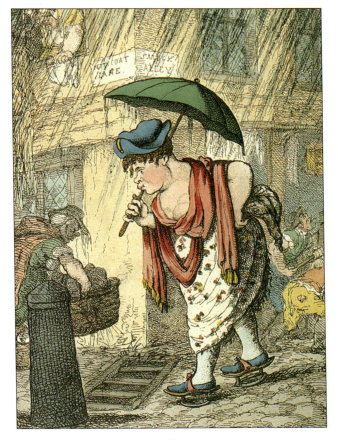

Snow-Bound

The sun that brief December day
   Rose cheerless over hills of grey,
And, darkly circled, gave at noon
   A sadder light than waning moon.
Slow tracing down the thickening sky
   Its mute and ominous prophecy,
A portent seeming less than threat,
   It sank from sight before it set.
A chill no coat, however stout,
   Of homespun stuff could quite shut out,
A hard, dull bitterness of cold,
   That checked, mid-vein, the circling race
Of life-blood in the sharpened face,
   The coming of the snow-storm told.

Unwarmed by any sunset light
   The grey day darkened into night,
A night made hoary with the swarm,
   And whirl-dance of the blinding storm.
And ere the early bed-time came
   The white drift piled the window-frame,
And through the glass the clothes-line posts
   Looked in like tall and sheeted ghosts.

JOHN GREENLEAF WHITTIER

A Christmas Banquet

HE DINNER WAS served up in the great hall, where the Squire always held his Christmas banquet. A blazing crackling fire of logs had been heaped on to warm the spacious apartment, and the flame went sparkling and wreathing up the wide-mouthed chimney. The great picture of the crusader and his white horse had been profusely decorated with greens for the occasion; and holly and ivy had likewise been wreathed round the helmet and weapons on the opposite wall....A sideboard was set out just under this chivalric trophy, on which was a display of plate that might have vied (at least in variety) with Belshazzar's parade of the vessels of the temple; 'flagons, cans, cups, beakers, goblets, basins, and ewers'; the gorgeous utensils of good companionship, that had gradually accumulated through many generations of jovial house-keepers. Before these stood the two Yule candles beaming like two stars of the first magnitude; other lights were distributed in branches, and the whole array glittered like a firmament of silver. We were ushered into this banqueting scene with the sound of minstrelsy, the old harper being seated on a stool beside the fireplace, and twanging his instrument with a vast deal more power than melody.

WASHINGTON IRVING

Days of Sombre Hue

The trees are bare, the sun is cold,
   And seldom, seldom seen;
The heavens have lost their zone of gold
   The earth its robe of green;

And ice upon the glancing stream
   Has cast its sombre shade,
And distant hills and valleys seem
   In frozen mist arrayed.

EMILY BRONTE

In a drear-nighted December,
   Too happy, happy tree,
Thy branches ne'er remember
   Their green felicity:
The north cannot undo them,
   With a sleety whistle through them;
Nor frozen thawings glue them
   From budding at the prime.

JOHN KEATS

The Thames Under Ice

HE FROST continuing more and more severe, the [frozen] Thames before London was still planted with booths in formal streets, all sorts of trades and shops furnished, and full of commodities, even to a printing press, where the people and ladies took a fancy to have their names printed, and the day and year set down when printed on the Thames. This humour took so universally that it was estimated the printer gained £5 a day for printing a line only, at sixpence a name, besides what he got by ballads, etc. Coaches plied from Westminster to the Temple, and from several other stairs to and fro, as in the streets, sleds, sliding with skates, a bull-baiting, horse and coach-races, puppet-plays and interludes, cooks, tippling, and other lewd places, so that it seemed to be a bacchanalian triumph, or carnival on the water, whilst it was a severe judgment on the land, the trees not only splitting, as if lightning-struck, but men and cattle perishing in diverse places, and the very seas so locked up with ice, that no vessel could stir out or come in. The fowls, fish and birds, and all our exotic plants and greens, universally perishing. Many parks of deer were destroyed, and all sorts of fuel so dear, that there were great contributions to preserve the poor alive.

JOHN EVELYN, 1684

Winter Song

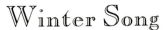

Ask me more, my truth to prove,
　　What I would suffer for my love.
With thee I would in exile go
　　To regions of eternal snow,
O'er floods by solid ice confined,
　　Through forest bare with northern wind;
While all around my eyes I cast,
　　Where all is wild and all is waste,
If there the tim'rous stag you chase,
　　Or rouse to fight a fiercer race,
Undaunted I thy arms would bear,
　　And give thy hand the hunter's spear.
When the low sun withdraws his light,
　　And menaces an half-year's night,
The conscious moon and stars above,
　　Shall guide me with my wand'ring love.
Beneath the mountain's hollow brow,
　　Or in its rocky cells below,
Thy rural feast I would provide,
　　Nor envy palaces their pride.

JAMES THOMSON

Degrees Below

HE FIRST WEEK in December was very wet, with the barometer very low. On the 7th, with the barometer at 28 – five tenths, came on a vast snow, which continued all that day and the next, and most part of the following night; so that by the morning of the 9th the works of men were quite overwhelmed, the lanes filled so as to be impassable, and the ground covered twelve or fifteen inches without any drifting. In the evening of the 9th the air began to be so very sharp that we thought it would be curious to attend to the motions of a thermometer. We therefore hung out two; one made by Martin and one by Dollond, which soon began to show us what we were to expect; for, by ten o'clock, they fell to 21, and at eleven to 4, when we went to bed. On the 10th, in the morning, the quicksilver of Dollond's glass was down to half a degree below zero and that of Martin's, which was absurdly graduated only to four degrees above zero, sunk quite into the brass guard of the ball; so that when the weather became most interesting this was useless. On the 10th, at eleven at night, though the air was perfectly still, Dolland's glass went down to one degree below zero!

GILBERT WHITE

Sources and Acknowledgments

For permission to reproduce illustrations, the publishers thank the following: Mary Evans Picture Library, Spink & Son Ltd., Manchester City Art Galleries and Sam Elder.